Something
to do
Something
to love
Something
to hope for

The grand essentials to happiness in this life
are something to do, something to love, and
something to hope for.

Joseph Addison

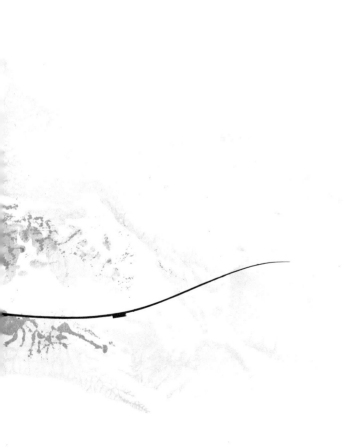

Something
to do
Something
to love
Something
to hope for

Compiled by Caesar Johnson

Designed by Gordon Brown

Published by The C. R. Gibson Company

Contents

Something to do

Happiness is a rebound from hard work. One of the follies of man
is to assume that he can enjoy mere emotion. As well try to
eat beauty! Happiness must be tricked. She loves to see men work.
She loves sweat, weariness, self-sacrifice. She will not be found
in palaces but lurking in cornfields and factories and on over
littered desks. She crowns the unconscious head of the busy man.

David Grayson

All happiness depends on courage and work. I have had many
periods of wretchedness, but with energy and above all, with
illusions, I pulled through them all.

Honoré de Balzac

Doing easily what others find difficult is talent; doing what is
impossible for talent is genius.

Henri-Frédéric Amiel

Happiness is in the taste, and not in the things themselves;
we are happy from possessing what we like,
not from possessing what others like.

François de La Rochefoucauld

Life is like playing the violin in public and learning the
instrument as one goes on.

Samuel Butler

When I hear somebody sigh that "Life is hard," I am always tempted
to ask, "Compared to what?"

Sydney Harris

I knew a woman once. A Philadelphia gentlewoman of eighty-seven summers. Each morning she would play three sets of tennis. True, she didn't win often. Her limbs were quite stiff as sometimes happens to older people. But to see her old-fashioned bloomers flapping gaily in the bright morning sunlight and hear her little shrieks of delight as she followed the ball from one side of the court to the other gave all of us pangs of joy. She was enjoying life and giving all of us renewed faith in ourselves in the offing!

What was this strange secret of happiness this aging heiress of an old Main Line family had discovered? What was it that drew men, one eighth her age, toward her? It was simply that she had found something outside herself! Through it she had found happiness, popularity, fame (in a local way, of course), and a new lease on life. In her case she had found a tennis ball.

You can do the same. Not a tennis ball necessarily. But something!

Richard Mathison

He who enjoys doing and enjoys what he has done is happy.

Johann Wolfgang von Goethe

To accomplish great things, we must not only act but also dream, not only plan but also believe.

Anatole France

The supply of time is a daily miracle. You wake up in the morning and lo! Your purse is magnificently filled with 24 hours of the unmanufactured tissue of the universe of life. It is yours! The most precious of your possessions.

Arnold Bennett

Great minds have purposes, others have wishes.

Washington Irving

The darkest hour in any man's life is when he sits down to plan how to get money without earning it.

Horace Greeley

I don't know who my grandfather was; I am much more concerned
to know what his grandson will be.

Abraham Lincoln

Work

Let me but do my work from day to day,
In field or forest, at the desk or loom.
In roaring market-place or tranquil room;
Let me but find it in my heart to say
When vagrant wishes beckon me astray,
"This is my work; my blessing, not my doom;
Of all who live, I am the one by whom
This work can best be done in the right way."

Then shall I see it not too great, nor small,
To suit my spirit and to prove my powers;
Then shall I cheerful greet the laboring hours,
And cheerful turn when the long shadows fall
At eventide, to play and love and rest,
Because I know for me my work is best.

Henry van Dyke

He has half the deed done, who has made a beginning.

Quintus Horatius Flaccus

Doing is the great thing. For if, resolutely, people do what is
right, in time they come to like doing it.

John Ruskin

The wise does at once what the fool does at last.

Baltasar Gracián

What you can become you are already.

Friedrich Hebbel

The man who does his work, any work, conscientiously, must always
be in one sense a great man.

Dinah Maria Mulock

What is this life, if full of care
We have no time to stand and stare.

No time to stand beneath the boughs
And stare as long as sheep or cows.

No time to see, when woods we pass,
Where squirrels hide their nuts in grass.

No time to see, in broad daylight,
Streams full of stars, like stars at night.

No time to turn at Beauty's glance,
And watch her feet, how they can dance.

No time to wait till her mouth can
Enrich that smile her eyes began.

A poor life this if, full of care,
We have no time to stand and stare.

William Henry Davies

Happiness is activity.

Aristotle

If we begin with certainties, we shall end in doubts;
but if we begin with doubts, and are patient in them,
we shall end in certainties.

Francis Bacon

My Creed

I would be true, for there are those who trust me;
I would be pure, for there are those who care;
I would be strong, for there is much to suffer;
I would be brave, for there is much to dare.
I would be friend of all — the poor — the friendless;
I would be giving and forget the gift;
I would be humble, for I know my weakness;
I would look up — and laugh — and love — and lift.

Howard Arnold Walter

Life's Mirror

There are loyal hearts, there are spirits brave,
There are souls that are pure and true;
Then give to the world the best you have,
And the best will come back to you.

Give love, and love to your life will flow,
A strength in your utmost need;
Have faith, and a score of hearts will show
Their faith in your word and deed.

Mary Ainge de Vere

To him whose elastic and vigorous thought keeps pace with the sun,
the day is a perpetual morning.

Henry David Thoreau

It is easier to fight for our principles than it is
to live up to them.

Alfred Adler

I desire so to conduct the affair of this administration
that if at the end, when I come to lay down the reins of power,
I have lost every other friend on earth, I shall at least have
one friend left, and that friend shall be down inside of me.

Abraham Lincoln

Man's happiness does not lie in freedom, but in acceptance of duty.

André Gide

Why not go out on a limb? Isn't that where the fruit is?

Frank Scully

Man is preeminently a creative animal, predestined to strive
consciously for an object and to engage in engineering — that is,
incessantly and eternally to make new roads, wherever they
may lead.

Feodor Dostoyevsky

13

Fish Can't Even Read or Write

Ten million people are planning to go fishing this summer. One million of them are already spending many hours over the selection of fancy lures, lines and rods, or exhausting themselves learning how to drop a fly lightly in the water so that it won't sink.

When they actually go fishing they will probably have no luck until they get a snarl in their line. While they are unsnarling it the fly will sink and a three-pound trout will grab the fly and catch himself. This will disconcert the angler, who thinks fish ought to play according to the rules.

An additional five million anglers are pondering over the colors of their casting plugs and arguing about the tints that fishes like best. But fishes are color-blind.

Millions of fishermen are examining flies under magnifying glasses to be sure they are exact replicas of living flies; more are testing plugs in the bathtub to find one that has the closest possible approach, in action, to the movements of the fish it is supposed to represent.

But fishes bite best on flies that have no counterpart in nature, and the deadliest casting lure ever invented is the common spoon hook, which looks like nothing on earth — or in its waters — other than a spoon hook.

Anglers are prone to regard fishes as their mental superiors, and in this way the lives of innumerable fishes are saved. The expression in a fish's eyes is no smoke screen hiding a Harvard intellect. Anglers who are now planning a scientific campaign against the fish would do well to spend a few hours in a fish market, looking at the fishes. They are just as dumb as they look. When treated as a fish, the fish is easy prey.

A fellow I know once caught a big trout which lay in a creek directly under a bridge. My friend first drifted a dry fly under the bridge, then a wet fly. He caught a grasshopper and tried that. No luck. Then the doughty angler figured that he had been drifting his lures downstream and the trout could see the line. So he performed the difficult feat of casting beneath the bridge, the lure striking the water just in front of the trout. But the trout paid no attention. As the angler cast again, his reel dropped off and sank to the bottom. Quick as a flash, the fish turned, swooped down on the reel and grabbed it.

My friend nearly landed him before he let go. If you really want to be a smart angler, you have to be dumb like a fish.

14

In every stream there is a deep pool in which lives a legendary fish, regarded as a combination of heavyweight champion and Rhodes scholar. His name is One Fin, Old Spotted Tail or Old Something Else. Every week some leading local angler tries his luck —and an infinite variety of scientific lures — with him. Sometimes the fish is hooked and lost. Sometimes he won't bite. You can see him down there reading Shakespeare, but he is too "wary," too smart to be caught.

Sometimes this grandpapa of all the fishes disappears. That is a sure sign that some kid has come along with a bunch of big angle-worms or a chunk of bacon on a hook big enough to catch Moby Dick, and has hauled him out.

Old Spotted Tail has a good reason for not biting on fancy flies. It takes about as much energy for a large fish to rise to the surface of a pool and return to its depths as a single fly supplies. A six-pound fish that kept chasing No. 16 flies would soon be a four-pound fish. To put it another way, a man who walked a block every day to eat a peanut would die of exhaustion quicker than one who sat on the curbstone and ate nothing.

The kid comes along with a hunk of bacon. Old Split Fin is lying deep in the pool because he is interested in food that is heavy enough to sink. He never saw a piece of bacon before, but it is his size and he goes for it.

Men have too much imagination to be good fishermen. They place themselves in the position of the fishes and select lures they would go for if they were fishes. It irks them to look upon fishing as a simple exercise undertaken by simple men and simpler fishes. They like to feel that when they have caught a fish they have overcome tremendous obstacles.

Try to look at the fish as he really is. He has just sufficient brain power to open his mouth when he sees something to eat, and to swallow it if it turns out all right or to wiggle his tail away from there if it does not. He does not know what a fishhook is, or a line or a leader. He is color-blind — scientifically established — and he will bite on anything that moves and on most things that stand still. When you come home with a big string of fishes, don't swell with pride. You have not caught the fishes; they have caught themselves.

Donald Hough

Win as if you were used to it, lose as if you
enjoyed it for a change.

Eric Mark Golnik

Those only are happy who have their minds fixed on some object
other than their own happiness; on the happiness of others, on the
improvement of mankind, even on some art or pursuit followed not
as a means but as itself an ideal end. Aiming thus at something else,
they find happiness by the way. . . . Ask yourself whether you are
happy, and you cease to be so. The only chance is to treat, not
happiness, but some end external to it, as the purpose of life.

John Stuart Mill

The Road Not Taken

Two roads diverged in a yellow wood,
And sorry I could not travel both
And be one traveler, long I stood
And looked down one as far as I could
To where it bent in the undergrowth;

Then took the other, as just as fair,
And having perhaps the better claim,
Because it was grassy and wanted wear;
Though as for that, the passing there
Had worn them really about the same.

And both that morning equally lay
In leaves no step had trodden black.
Oh, I kept the first for another day!
Yet knowing how way leads on to way,
I doubted if I ever should come back.

I shall be telling this with a sigh
Somewhere ages and ages hence:
Two roads diverged in a wood, and I —
I took the one less traveled by,
And that has made all the difference.

Robert Frost

Preparedness

For all your days prepare,
    And meet them ever alike:
When you are the anvil, bear—
    When you are the hammer, strike.

Edwin Markham

Shun idleness, it is the rust that attaches itself
to the most brilliant metals.

Voltaire

The only man who never makes mistakes
is the man who never does anything.

Theodore Roosevelt

A life of ease is a difficult pursuit.

William Cowper

Whatever is worth doing at all, is worth doing well.

Lord Chesterfield

It take less time to do a thing right
than it does to explain why you did it wrong.

Henry Wadsworth Longfellow

Genius is one per cent inspiration
and ninety-nine per cent perspiration.

Thomas A. Edison

God loves to help him who strives to help himself.

Aeschylus

There are obviously two educations. One should teach us
how to make a living. The other should teach us how to live.

James Truslow Adams

Folk want a lot of loving every minute —
The sympathy of others and their smile!
Till life's end, from the moment they begin it,
Folks need a lot of loving all the while.

Strickland Gillilan

There is so much good in the worst of us,
And so much bad in the best of us,
That it ill behoves any of us
To find fault with the rest of us.

Unknown

As a general rule the most successful man in life
is the man who has the best information.

Benjamin Disraeli

Genius is the capacity for taking infinite pains.

Thomas Carlyle

Before everything else, getting ready is the secret of success.

Henry Ford

Preparation

We're never done preparing. Every act we perform, even if it seems at the time practically our whole purpose in life, is really nothing but preparation for something we'll do at some future time. So long as we live we're never done. Today prepares for tomorrow, and next year prepares for the year after it. Our life is a sort of savings bank in which we deposit our acts and our experiences to use when we need them — and we always need them. Someone once said that we don't live long enough to learn enough to make ourselves really useful. Just the same, the more we learn and the more we prepare, the nearer we are to usefulness. So don't be discouraged because life is nothing but a series of preparations. It would be terribly dull if we came to a time when there was nothing else for which to prepare.

Unknown

What on earth would a man do with himself
if something did not stand in his way?

H. G. Wells

I start where the last man left off.

Thomas A. Edison

Lifting and Leaning

There are two kinds of people on earth today,
Just two kinds of people, no more, I say.

Not the good and the bad, for 'tis well understood
The good are half bad and the bad are half good.

Not the happy and sad, for the swift-flying years
Bring each man his laughter and each man his tears.

Not the rich and the poor, for to count a man's wealth
You must first know the state of his conscience and health.

Not the humble and proud, for in life's busy span
Who puts on vain airs is not counted a man.

No! the two kinds of people on earth I mean
Are the people who lift and the people who lean.

Wherever you go you will find the world's masses
Are ever divided in just these two classes.

And strangely enough, you will find, too, I ween,
There is only one lifter to twenty who lean.

In which class are you? Are you easing the load
Of overtaxed lifters who toil down the road?

Or are you a leaner who lets others bear
Your portion of worry and labor and care?

Ella Wheeler Wilcox

In this world it is not what we take up,
but what we give up, that makes us rich.

Henry Ward Beecher

To a Friend

You entered my life in a casual way,
And saw at a glance what I needed;
There were others who passed me or met me each day,
But never a one of them heeded.
Perhaps you were thinking of other folks more,
Or chance simply seemed to decree it;
I know there were many such chances before,
But the others — well, they didn't see it.

You said just the thing that I wished you would say,
And you made me believe that you meant it;
I held up my head in the old gallant way,
And resolved you should never repent it.
There are times when encouragement means such a lot,
And a word is enough to convey it;
There were others who could have, as easy as not —
But, just the same, they didn't say it.

There may have been someone who could have done more
To help me along, though I doubt it;
What I needed was cheering, and always before
They had let me plod on without it.
You helped to refashion the dream of my heart,
And made me turn eagerly to it;
There were others who might have (I question that part) —
But, after all, they didn't do it!

Grace Stricker Dawson

To avoid criticism, do nothing, say nothing, be nothing.

Elbert Hubbard

It is better to know nothing than to know what ain't so.

Josh Billings

Not only strike while the iron is hot, but make it hot by striking.

Oliver Cromwell

20

He who knows not, and knows not that he knows not,
    is a fool, shun him;
He who knows not, and knows that he knows not,
    is a child, teach him.
He who knows, and knows not that he knows
    is asleep, wake him.
He who knows, and knows that he knows,
    is wise, follow him.

Proverb

Diligence is the mother of good luck.

Benjamin Franklin

Do not pray for easy lives. Pray to be stronger men!

Phillips Brooks

No good fish goes anywhere without a porpoise.

Lewis Carroll

Success

Success is speaking words of praise,
In cheering other people's ways,
In doing just the best you can,
With every task and every plan,
It's silence when your speech would hurt,
Politeness when your neighbor's curt,
It's deafness when the scandal flows,
And sympathy with others' woes,
It's loyalty when duty calls,
It's courage when disaster falls,
It's patience when the hours are long,
It's found in laughter and in song,
It's in the silent time of prayer,
In happiness and in despair,
In all of life and nothing less,
We find the thing we call success.

Unknown

Tell Him So

If you hear a kind word spoken
Of some worthy soul you know,
It may fill his heart with sunshine
If you only tell him so.

If a deed, however humble,
Helps you on your way to go,
Seek the one whose hand has helped you,
Seek him out and tell him so!

If your heart is touched and tender
Toward a sinner lost and low,
It might help him to do better
If you'd only tell him so!

Oh, my sisters, oh, my brothers,
As o'er life's rough path you go,
If God's love has saved and kept you,
Do not fail to tell men so!

Unknown

Even a fool, when he holdeth his peace, is counted wise.

Proverbs 17:28

A bore is a person who talks when you want him to listen.

Ambrose Bierce

Some folks are wise and some otherwise.

English Aphorism

A Wise Old Owl

A wise old owl lived in an oak;
The more he saw the less he spoke;
The less he spoke the more he heard:
Why can't we all be like that bird?

Edward Hersey Richards

Children think not of what is past, nor what is to come,
but enjoy the present time, which few of us do.

Jean de La Bruyère

Adventure is not outside a man; it is within.

David Grayson

Don't Die On Third

It was several weeks ago, when the Tigers were playing the team from Cleveland. Moriarty was on third base.

Around the chalk-lined arena 18,000 persons strained themselves in tense expectancy. The score was a tie. Two men were out. The fate of the game centered in the white-bloused figure that shuttled back and forth near third. Tigers and Nats stood up at their benches, for the decisive moment had come.

Moriarty was at third.

He got there by the ordinary events of the game. At the bat he hit the ball and ran to first. Another player bunted and sacrificed himself to run Moriarty to second. Then a long fly advanced him to third. There he stood, alert and active, with the fate of the game in his quick eye, his quicker brain, and his running legs.

If he failed, he failed not alone, for the team failed with him. If he won, he won not alone, but gave the men behind him their chance for home. In him centered the hopes and fears of thousand upon thousand of spectators who had forgotten to breathe, and so still was the park that even the breeze seemed forgetful to blow.

Moriarty was at third.

Much as it meant to have advanced that far, nothing had been accomplished by it. Three-quarter runs are not marked up on the score boards. Third-base runs never raised a pennant.

Third base is not a destination, but the last little way station on the road home. It is better not to run at all than to run to third and die. The 18,000 spectators that kept ominously silent at that moment could be changed into a vortex of cheering hero-worshippers or into an animated groan by the kind of work a man did between third and home.

There is no time for self-congratulation on third. The question is how to get safely away from it. The man on second wants your place— he can get it, but if you get safely home no one can take that achievement from you. One way to get off third is to wait for some fellow to bat you off; another way is to get away on your own initiative and according to your own secret plan.

Moriarty was on third.

It is ninety feet from third to home. Sometimes that ninety feet is a leaden mile, sometimes a mere patter of lightning-like steps. If it is a mile to you, you are a failure, and the great circle of spectators groan for your incompetency; if it is but a lightning streak, you are the great man of the baseball day. Moriarty was intent on dwindling that ninety feet instead of lengthening it.

How many things converged into the few moments he stood there. He watched the signals of the Cleveland catcher — he gathered they meant a high ball. A high ball meant that the runner might duck low to the base while the catcher's hands were in the air after the ball. Moriarty knew, too, that a high ball required that the pitcher wind up his arm in a certain way. He knew, also, that pitchers have a way of winding up when they don't intend to throw the ball. More than that he knew the pitcher in the box was left-handed and could not keep his eyes on third when winding up. That was why Moriarty closely followed all the strange little signals pitcher and catcher were making.

There was another consideration, too — Mullin was up to bat. Moriarty knows that Mullin has a batting average of something like .250, which means that Mullin hits safely about once in four times at bat. Would the ball about to be thrown be one of the hit or one of the missed? No human calculation could even guess at that. If Mullin missed, it would be useless for Moriarty to run. If Mullin hit, there were still chances of his being put out at first, and ending the inning.

There was only one thing to do — make home between the time the pitcher wound up his arm past all recall and the time the ball landed in the catcher's glove — make home in the hope that Mullin would either reach first safely or that he would not strike at that ball.

It was to be a contest of speed between a five-ounce ball delivered with all the force of a superb pitching arm and the one hundred and seventy pound body of Moriarty. An unequal contest at that, for the five-ounce ball travels only sixty feet while the runner from third must hurl his body over a distance of ninety feet.

All these considerations are in the mind of Moriarty. He builds up his prospective run as an engineer builds a bridge over a torrent, step by step with infinite pains. Now the Cleveland pitcher is winding up his arm — round and round it swings — he poises himself — there is yet a fraction of a second in which he can recall his intended throw — Moriarty is crouched like a tiger about to spring. Now! Now!

There is a white streak across the field! A cloud of dust at the home plate! The umpire stands with his hands extended, palms down.

A bursting roar of acclaim echoes and re-echoes across the space of the park. Again and again it bursts forth in thrilling electric power. Thirty-six thousand eyes strain toward the man who is slapping the dust from his white uniform.

Moriarty is home!

The Detroit News

Our main business is not to see what lies dimly at a distance
but to do what lies clearly at hand.

Thomas Carlyle

A conservative is a man who is too cowardly to fight
and too fat to run.

Elbert Hubbard

It is impossible to enjoy idling thoroughly unless one has
plenty of work to do.

Jerome K. Jerome

We have forty million reasons for failure, but not a single excuse.

Rudyard Kipling

By the street of By-and-By, one arrives at the house of Never.

Miguel de Cervantes

The saints are the sinners who keep trying.

Robert Louis Stevenson

A brook is going somewhere. It is water-on-a-mission. About to present itself to other waters at its destination, it never neglects little wayside opportunities. On its way to make its final offering, it gaily gives itself all along the way. Deer drink of its refreshing coolness with a deep content. Boys of seven years and of seventy probe its pools and eddies with their lures and return home at day's end with the brook's gift of speckled trout. Fish, crustaceans, mollusks, and water insects are given a home in its swirling currents and tranquil pools. From its birth in the bubbling springs to its arrival at its final goal the brook is selfless and a happy appearing thing. Service and happiness belong together.

Harold E. Kohn

All service ranks the same with God — There is no last nor first.

Robert Browning

The less one has to do, the less time one finds to do it in.

Lord Chesterfield

Money and time are the heaviest burdens of life,
and the unhappiest of all mortals are those who have more of
either than they know how to use.

Samuel Johnson

They fail, and they alone, who have not striven.

T. B. Aldrich

26

Our greatest glory is not in never falling
but in rising every time we fall.

Confucius

Consider the postage stamp, my son. It secures success through
its ability to stick to one thing till it gets there.

Josh Billings

A wise man who stands firm is a statesman,
a foolish man who stands firm is a catastrophe.

Adlai Stevenson

Half our mistakes in life arise from feeling where we ought to
think, and thinking where we ought to feel.

John Churton Collins

The art of being wise is the art of knowing what to overlook.

William James

If an animal does something they call it instinct.
If we do exactly the same thing for the same reason
they call it intelligence. I guess what they mean is that we
all make mistakes, but intelligence
enables us to do it on purpose.

Will Cuppy

When we cannot find contentment in ourselves, it is useless
to seek it elsewhere.

François de La Rochefoucauld

The reason a lot of people do not recognize an opportunity when
they meet it is that it usually goes around wearing overalls
and looking like hard work.

Unknown

Something to love

And the Lord God caused a deep sleep to fall upon Adam, and he slept: and he took one of his ribs, and closed up the flesh instead thereof; and the rib, which the Lord God had taken from man, made he a woman, and brought her unto the man. And Adam said, This is now bone of my bones, and flesh of my flesh: she shall be called Woman, because she was taken out of man. Therefore shall a man leave his father and mother, and shall cleave unto his wife: and they shall be one flesh.

Genesis 2:21-24

What else
Is love, but the most noble, pure affection
Of what is truly beautiful and fair,
Desire of union with the thing beloved?
I have read somewhere, that man and woman
Were, in the first creation, both one piece,
And being cleft asunder, ever since
Love was an appetite to be rejoined.

Ben Jonson

My bounty is as boundless as the sea,
My love as deep; the more I give to thee
The more I have, for both are infinities.

William Shakespeare

I have now come to the conclusion never again to think of marrying, and for this reason — I can never be satisfied with anyone who would be blockhead enough to have me.

Abraham Lincoln

We Have Lived and Loved Together

We have lived and loved together
Through many changing years;
We have shared each other's gladness
And wept each other's tears;
I have known ne'er a sorrow
That was long unsoothed by thee;
For thy smiles can make a summer
Where darkness else would be.

Like the leaves that fall around us
In autumn's fading hours,
Are the traitor's smiles, that darken
When the cloud of sorrow lowers;
And though many such we've known, love,
Too prone, alas, to range,
We both can speak of one love
Which time can never change.

We have lived and loved together
Through many changing years,
We have shared each other's gladness
And wept each other's tears.
And let us hope the future
As the past has been will be:
I will share with thee my sorrows,
And thou thy joys with me.

Charles Jefferys

A wise woman will always let her husband have her way.

Richard Sheridan

Let the man who does not wish to be idle fall in love.

Ovid

Many waters cannot quench love, neither can the floods drown it.

Song of Solomon 8:7

A Love Letter
John Jay Chapman to his Wife

I have sealed up each one of these letters thinking I had done —
and then a wave of happiness has come over me — remembering
you — only you — and the joy of life. Where were you, since
the beginning of the world? But now you are here, about me in
every space, room, sunlight, with your heart and arms and
the light of your soul — and the strong vigor of your presence.

Is love a hand or a foot — is it a picture or a poem or a fireside —
is it a compact or a permission or eagles that meet in the
clouds — No, no, no, no. It is light and heat and hand and foot
and ego. If I take the wings of the morning and remain in
the uttermost parts of the sea, there art thou also. What matter is
it what else the world contains — if you only are in it in every
part of it? I can find no corner of it without you — my eyes
would not see it. It is empty — I have seen all that there is
and it is nothing, and over creation are your wings.

We must be written in the book of the blessed. We have had
what life could give, we have eaten of the tree of knowledge, we
have known — we have been the mystery of the universe. I
wonder we do not shine — or speak with every gesture and accent
giving messages from the infinite. I wonder people do not
look after us in the street as if they had seen an angel.

Your John

Those who love deeply never grow old; they may die of old age,
but they die young.

Sir Arthur Pinero

To be in love is merely to be in a state of perpetual anaesthesis.

H. L. Mencken

We don't believe in rheumatism and true love
until after the first attack.

Marie Enber-Eschnenbach

31

Tell Her So

Amid the cares of married life,
In spite of toil and business strife,
If you value your sweet wife,
    Tell her so!

Prove to her you don't forget
The bond to which your seal is set;
She's of life's sweet the sweetest yet—
    Tell her so!

Don't act as if she'd passed her prime,
As though to please her was a crime—
If e'er you loved her, now's the time:
    Tell her so!

Never let her heart grow cold—
Richer beauties will unfold;
She is worth her weight in gold

                    Unknown

Every woman is wrong until she cries,
and then she is right, instantly.

                    Thomas Chandler Haliburton

The pleasure of love is in the loving. We are happier
in the passion we feel than in that we inspire.

                    François de La Rochefoucauld

Love is the state in which man sees things most decidedly
as they are not.

                    Friedrich Nietzsche

Love comes unseen; we only see it go.

                    Austin Dobson

Love is the whole history of a woman's life.

                    Madame de Staël

When I was a young man I vowed never to marry until I found
the ideal woman. Well, I found her — but, alas, she was
waiting for the ideal man.

Robert Schumann

Pains of love be sweeter far
Than all other pleasures are.

John Dryden

If we spend our lives in loving, we have no leisure to complain,
or to feel unhappiness.

Joseph Joubert

Song

O, let the solid ground
Not fail beneath my feet
Before my life has found
What some have found so sweet;
Then let come what come may,
What matter if I go mad,
I shall have had my day.

Let the sweet heavens endure,
Not close and darken above me
Before I am quite, quite sure
That there is one to love me!
Then let come what come may
To a life that has been so sad,
I shall have had my day.

Alfred, Lord Tennyson

The supreme happiness of life is the conviction of being loved
for yourself, or, more correctly, being loved in spite of yourself.

Victor Hugo

To live is like to love — all reason is against it,
and all healthy instinct for it.

Samuel Butler

Woodrow Wilson to Ellen Axson
During Their Courtship

October 16, 1883
Baltimore, Maryland

. . . How I wish that I could write you tonight such a letter as I should like to write; but it seems as if my love for you were literally unspeakable . . . Thoughts of you fill my life. You seem to be in everything I read, in everything I do. I can't enjoy myself without wishing that you might share the enjoyment; I can't read anything that is stimulating or eloquent or instructive without wishing that I might share it with you. I involuntarily smile in sympathy with anyone who seems happy, because I am happy; I pity everyone who seems downcast because I imagine that they are not loved by those whom they love. I am fast losing all semblance of a reputation for dignity because of the way I frolic and joke and rejoice in the manufacture of light-hearted nonsense when I am with my friends. I feel as if I should like very much to repeat poetry all the time — if I knew any to repeat. I am in a fair way to be run away with by this love that has taken possession of me. If you continue to love me and write me such elating letters I don't know what will become of this hitherto respectable person!

To love and win is the best thing; to love and lose, the next best.

William Makepeace Thackeray

He who is not impatient is not in love.

Pietro Aretino

Love is said to be blind, but I know lots of fellows in love who can see twice as much in their sweethearts as I can.

Josh Billings

I should like to see any kind of a man, distinguishable from a gorilla, that some good and even pretty woman could not shape a husband out of.

Oliver Wendell Holmes

Marriage is a mistake of youth — which we should all make.

Don Herold

Jenny Kissed Me

Jenny kissed me when we met,
Jumping from the chair she sat in.
Time, you thief! who love to get
Sweets into your list, put that in.
Say I'm weary, say I'm sad;
Say that health and wealth have missed me;
Say I'm growing old, but add—
                    Jenny kissed me!

Leigh Hunt

Generally the woman chooses the man who will choose her.

Paul Geraldy

The fickleness of the woman I love is only equaled
by the infernal constancy of the women who love me.

George Bernard Shaw

Boys will be boys — and so will a lot of middle-aged men.

Kin Hubbard

Love all God's creation, the whole and every grain of sand in it.
Love every leaf, every ray of God's light. Love the animals, love
the plants, love everything. If you love everything, you will perceive
the divine mystery in things. Once you perceive it, you will begin
to comprehend it better every day, and you will come at last to
love the whole world with an all-embracing love. Love the animals:
God has given them the rudiments of thought and joy untroubled.
Do not trouble it, don't harass them, don't deprive them of their
happiness, don't work against God's intent. Love children especially,
for they too are sinless like the angels; they live to soften and
purify our hearts and as it were guide us.

Feodor Dostoyevsky

To My Dear And Loving Husband

If ever two were one, then surely we;
If ever man were loved by wife, then thee;
If ever wife was happy in a man,
Compare with me, ye women, if you can.
I prize thy love more than whole mines of gold,
Or all the riches that the East doth hold.
My love is such that rivers cannot quench,
Nor aught but love from thee give recompense.
Thy love is such I can no way repay;
The heavens reward thee manifold, I pray.
Then while we live in love let's so persevere
That when we live no more we may live ever.

Anne Bradstreet

She Walks in Beauty

She walks in beauty like the night
Of cloudless climes and starry skies;
And all that's best of dark and bright
Meets in her aspect and her eyes:
Thus mellow'd to that tender light
Which heaven to gaudy day denies.

One shade the more, one ray the less,
Had half impair'd the nameless grace
Which waves in every raven tress,
Or softly lightens o'er her face—
Where thoughts serenely sweet express
How pure, how dear their dwelling-place.

And on that cheek, and o'er that brow,
So soft, so calm, yet eloquent,
The smiles that win, the tints that glow,
But tell of days in goodness spent,
A mind at peace with all below,
A heart whose love is innocent.

George Gordon, Lord Byron

Song

Not from the whole wide world I chose thee—
Sweetheart, light of the land and the sea!
The wide, wide world could not enclose thee,
For thou art the whole wide world to me.

Richard Watson Gilder

The dearest thing to a married man should be his wife but it is
not infrequently her clothes.

James Montgomery Bailey

Love iz like the meazles; we kant have it bad but onst,
and the later in life we have it the tuffer it goes with us.

Josh Billings

Endless torments dwell about thee: Yet who would live,
and live without thee!

Joseph Addison

Many a man has fallen in love with a girl in a light so dim
he would not have chosen a suit by it.

Maurice Chevalier

First love is a kind of vaccination which saves man
from catching the same complaint a second time.

Honoré de Balzac

The feller that puts off marryin' till he can support a wife
ain't very much in love.

Kin Hubbard

I would give up all my genius, and all my books,
if there were only some woman, somewhere,
who cared whether or not I came home late for dinner.

Ivan Turgenev

Song

Love's on the highroad,
Love's in the byroad—
Love's on the meadow, and Love's on the mart!
And down every byway
Where I have taken my way
I've met Love a-smiling — for Love's in my heart!

Dana Burnet

April's Amazing Meaning

April's amazing meaning doubtless lies
In tall, hoarse boys and slips
of slender girls with suddenly wider eyes
and parted lips;

For girls must wander pensive in the spring
When the green rain is over,
Doing some slow, inconsequential thing,
Plucking clover;

And any boy alone upon a bench
When his work's done will sit
And stare at the black ground and break a branch
And whittle it

Slowly; and boys and girls, irresolute,
Will curse the dreamy weather
Until they meet past the pale hedge and put
Their lips together.

George Dillon

Yes, Love indeed is light from heaven;
A spark of that immortal fire.

George Gordon, Lord Byron

A bit of fragrance always clings to the hand
that gives you roses.

Chinese Proverb

38

Momentous Words

What spiteful chance steals unawares
Wherever lovers come,
And trips the nimblest brain and scares
The bravest feelings dumb?

We had one minute at the gate,
Before the others came;
Tomorrow it would be too late,
And whose would be the blame!

I gazed at her, she glanced at me;
Alas! the time sped by:
"How warm it is today!" said she;
"It looks like rain," said I.

Edward Rowland Sill

Once we read Tennyson aloud
In our great fireside chair;
Between the lines my lips could touch
Her April-scented hair.

How very fond I was, to think
The printed poems fair,
When close within my arms I held
A living lyric there!

Christopher Morley

Opal

You are ice and fire,
The touch of you burns my hands like snow.
You are cold and flame.
You are the crimson of amaryllis,
The silver of moon-touched magnolias.
When I am with you,
My heart is a frozen pond
Gleaming with agitated torches.

Amy Lowell

Because

It is not because your heart is
      mine — mine only—
  Mine alone;
It is not because you chose me,
      weak and lonely,
  For your own;
Not because the earth is fairer,
      and the skies
  Spread above you
Are more radiant for the shining
      of your eyes—
  That I love you!

But because this human Love,
      though true and sweet—
  Yours and mine—
Has been sent by Love more tender,
      more complete,
  More divine;
That it leads our hearts to rest
      at last in Heaven,
  Far above you;
Do I take you as a gift that God
      has given—
  And I love you!

Adelaide Anne Proctor

What Is Once Loved

What is once loved
You will find
Is always yours
From that day.
Take it home
In your mind
And nothing ever
Can take it away.

Elizabeth Coatsworth

O, Love Is Not A Summer Mood

O, Love is not a summer mood,
   Nor flying phantom of the brain,
Nor youthful fever of the blood,
      Nor dream, nor fate, nor circumstance.
      Love is not born of blinded chance,
      Nor bred in simple ignorance.

Love is the flower of maidenhood;
   Love is the fruit of mortal pain;
And she hath winter in her blood.
      True love is steadfast as the skies,
      And once alight, she never flies;
      And love is strong, and love is wise.

Richard Watson Gilder

Since We Parted

Since we parted yester eve,
I do love thee, love, believe,
Twelve times dearer, twelve hours longer,—
One dream deeper, one night stronger,
One sun surer, — thus much more
Than I loved thee, love, before.

Edward Robert Bulwer-Lytton

I ask a moment's indulgence to sit by thy side. The works that I have in hand I will finish afterwards.

Away from the sight of thy face my heart knows no rest nor respite, and my work becomes an endless toil in a shoreless sea of toil.

To-day the summer has come at my window with its sighs and murmurs; and the bees are plying their minstrelsy at the court of the flowering grove.

Now it is the time to sit quiet, face to face with thee, and to sing dedication of life in this silent and overflowing leisure.

Rabindranath Tagore

Doubt thou the stars are fire;
Doubt thou that the sun doth move;
Doubt truth to be a liar,
But never doubt I love.

William Shakespeare

Love is the most terrible, and also the most generous of the passions;
it is the only one which includes in its dreams
the happiness of someone else.

Alphonse Karr

My April Lady

When down the stair at morning
    The sunbeams round her float,
Sweet rivulets of laughter
    Are rippling in her throat;
The gladness of her greeting
    Is gold without alloy;
And in the morning sunlight
    I think her name is Joy.

When in the evening twilight
    The quiet book-room lies,
We read the sad old ballads,
    While from her hidden eyes
The tears are falling, falling,
    That give her heart relief;
And in the evening twilight,
    I think her name is Grief.

My little April lady,
    Of sunshine and of showers
She weaves the old spring magic,
    And breaks my heart in flowers!
But when her moods are ended,
    She nestles like a dove;
Then, by the pain and rapture,
    I know her name is Love.

Henry van Dyke

Love in the Winds

When I am standing on a mountain crest,
Or hold the tiller in the dashing spray,
My love of you leaps foaming in my breast,
Shouts with the winds and sweeps to their foray;
My heart bounds with the horses of the sea,
And plunges in the wild ride of the night,
Flaunts in the teeth of tempest the large glee
That rides our Fate and welcomes gods to fight.
Ho, love, I laugh aloud for love of you,
Glad that our love is fellow to rough weather,—
No fretful orchid hothoused from the dew,
But hale and hardy as the highland heather,
Rejoicing in the wind that stings and thrills,
Comrade of ocean, playmate of the hills.

Richard Hovey

Love consists in this that two solitudes protect
and touch and greet each other.

Ranier Maria Rilke

To Husband and Wife

Preserve sacredly the privacies of your home, your married state
and your heart. Let no father or mother or sister or brother ever
presume to come between you or share the joys or sorrows that
belong to you two alone.

With mutual help build your quiet world, not allowing your
dearest earthly friend to be the confidant of aught that concerns
your domestic peace. Let moments of alienation, if they occur, be
healed at once. Never, no never, speak of it outside; but to each
other confess and all will come out right. Never let the morrow's
sun still find you at variance. Renew and renew your vow. It will do
you good; and thereby your minds will grow together contented in
that love which is stronger than death, and you will be truly one.

Margaret Springdale

Spray

I knew you thought of me all night,
I knew though you were far away;
I felt your love blow over me
As if a dark wind-riven sea
Drenched me with quivering spray.

There are so many ways to love
And each way has its own delights—
Then be content to come to me
Only as spray the beating sea
Drives inland through the night.

Sara Teasdale

When You Are Old

When you are old and gray and full of sleep,
And nodding by the fire, take down this book,
And slowly read, and dream of the soft look
Your eyes had once, and of their shadows deep;

How many loved your moments of glad grace,
And loved your beauty with love false or true;
But one man loved the pilgrim soul in you,
And loved the sorrows of your changing face.

And bending down beside the glowing bars
Murmur, a little sadly, how love fled
And paced upon the mountains overhead
And hid his face amid a crowd of stars.

William Butler Yeats

They gave each other a smile with a
Future in it.

Ring Lardner

No cord nor cable can so forcibly draw, or hold so fast,
as love can do with a twined thread.

Robert Burton

44

Song

Let my voice ring out and over the earth,
Through all the grief and strife,
With a golden joy in a silver mirth;
Thank God for life!

Let my voice swell out through the great abyss
To the azure dome above,
With a chord of faith in the harp of bliss:
Thank God for Love!

Let my voice thrill out beneath and above,
The whole world through:
O my love and life, O my life and love,
Thank God for you.

James Thomson

Marriage

Going my way of old
Contented more or less
I dreamt not life could hold
Such happiness.

I dreamt not that love's way
Could keep the golden height
Day after happy day,
Night after night.

Wilfrid Wilson Gibson

We don't get to know anything but what we love.

Johann Wolfgang von Goethe

A part of kindness consists in loving people more than they deserve.

Joseph Joubert

The way to love anything is to realize it might be lost.

G. K. Chesterton

A Love Letter by Mark Twain

My Dear, Dear Livy:

This day I prize above every gift so much of your precious love as I do possess and so am satisfied and happy. I feel no exacting spirit — I am grateful, grateful, unspeakably grateful for the love you have already given me. I am crowned — I am throned — I am sceptered. I sit with Kings.

I do love, love, love you, Livy! My whole being is permeated, is renewed, is leavened with this love and with every breath I draw its noble influence makes of me a better man. And I shall yet be worthy of your priceless love, Livy. It is the glad task of my life— it is the purest ambition and the most exalted that ever I have known, and I shall never, never swerve from the path it has marked out for me, while the goal and you are before me.

Goodbye, Livy. You are so pure, so great, so good, so beautiful. How can I help loving you? Say, rather, how can I keep from worshipping you, you dear little paragon. If I could only see you! I do wish I could. Write me im-mediately. Don't wait a minute. You are never out of my waking thoughts for a single fraction of a second, and I do want to hear from you.

Good-bye, Livy. All this time I have felt just as if you were here with me, almost — and part of the time as if I could see you standing by me. But you are vanished! I miss a gracious presence— a glory is gone from about me. I listen for a dear voice, I look for a darling face, I caress the empty air! God bless you, my idol. Good-bye, and I send you a thousand kisses — pray send me some.

Most lovingly, Yours
Forever — Samuel

God is love; and he that dwelleth in love
dwelleth in God, and God in him.

I John 4:16

46

My beloved spake, and said unto me,
Rise up, my love, my fair one, and come away.
For, lo, the winter is past,
The rain is over and gone;
The flowers appear on the earth;
The time of the singing of birds is come,
And the voice of the turtle is heard in our land;
The fig tree putteth forth her green figs,
And the vines with the tender grape
Give a good smell.
Arise, my love, my fair one, and come away.

The Song of Solomon 2:10-13

Talk to a man about himself and he will listen for hours.

Benjamin Disraeli

The way to be happy is to make others so.

Ralph Ingersoll

Love's Philosophy

The fountains mingle with the river
And the rivers with the ocean;
The winds of heaven mix forever
With a sweet emotion;
Nothing in the world is single;
All things by a law divine
In one spirit meet and mingle.
Why not I with thine?

See the mountains kiss high heaven,
And the waves clasp one another;
No sister-flower would be forgiven
If it disdained its brother;
And the sunlight clasps the earth,
And the moonbeams kiss the sea:
What are all these kissings worth
If thou kiss not me?

Percy Bysshe Shelley

Something to hope for

Everything in the world is done from hope.
No farmer would sow one grain
if he did not hope it would grow to seed.
No young man would take a wife if he didn't hope
to have children by her. No merchant or working man would work
if he didn't hope for profit or wages.
Then how much more hope calls us to eternal life.

Martin Luther

A heathen philosopher once asked a Christian,
"Where is God?" The Christian answered,
"Let me first ask you, Where is He not?"

Aaron Arrowsmith

Back of the loaf is the snowy flour,
And back of the flour the mill;
And back of the mill is the wheat, and the shower,
And the sun, and the Father's will.

Maltbie Babcock

Don't Give Up

'Twixt failure and success the point's so fine
Men sometime know not when they touch the line,
Just when the pearl was waiting one more plunge,
How many a struggler has thrown up the sponge!
Then take this honey from the bitterest cup:
"There is no failure save in giving up!"

Howard Dillingham

49

Optimism

Talk happiness. The world is sad enough
Without your woes. No path is wholly rough;
Look for the places that are smooth and clear,
And speak of those, to rest the weary ear
Of Earth, so hurt by one continuous strain
Of human discontent and grief and pain.

Talk faith. The world is better off without
Your uttered ignorance and morbid doubt.
If you have faith in God, or man, or self,
Say so. If not, push back upon the shelf
Of silence all your thoughts, till faith shall come;
No one will ever grieve because your lips are dumb.

Talk health. The dreary, never-changing tale
Of mortal maladies is worn and stale.
You cannot charm, or interest, or please
By harping on that minor chord, disease.
Say you are well, or all is well with you,
And God shall hear your words and make them true.

Ella Wheeler Wilcox

I am an old man and have known a great many troubles,
but most of them never happened.

Mark Twain

A simple, childlike faith in a Divine Friend solves all the
problems that come to us by land or sea.

Helen Keller

All things work together for good to them that love God.

Romans 8:28

There is not a heart but has its moments of longing,
yearning for something better, nobler, holier than it knows now.

Henry Ward Beecher

50

Make a joyful noise unto the Lord, all ye lands.

Serve the Lord with gladness: come before his presence with singing.

Know ye that the Lord he is God: it is he that hath made us, and not we ourselves; we are his people, and the sheep of his pasture.

Enter into his gates with thanksgiving, and into his courts with praise: be thankful unto him, and bless his name.

For the Lord is good; his mercy is everlasting; and his truth endureth to all generations.

Psalm 100

All human wisdom is summed up in two words — wait and hope.

Alexandre Dumas, père

All the great things are simple, and many can be expressed in a single word: freedom; justice; honor; duty; mercy; hope.

Winston S. Churchill

No man is useless while he has a friend.

Robert Louis Stevenson

One cannot always be a hero, but one can always be a man.

Johann Wolfgang von Goethe

Great hopes make great men.

Thomas Fuller

There is nothing on earth worth being known, but God and our own souls.

Gameliel Bailey

God hangs the greatest weights on the smallest wires.

Sir Fancis Bacon

Trust men, and they will be true to you; treat them greatly,
and they will show themselves great.

Ralph Waldo Emerson

You Have to Believe

You have to believe in happiness,
   Or happiness never comes.
I know that a bird chirps none the less
   When all that he finds is crumbs.
You have to believe the buds will blow
Believe in the grass in the days of snow;
   Ah, that's the reason a bird can sing—
   On his darkest day he believes in Spring.

You have to believe in happiness—
   It isn't an outward thing.
The Spring never makes the song, I guess,
   As much as the song the Spring.
Aye, many a heart could find content
If it saw the joy on the road it went
   The joy ahead when it had to grieve—
   For the joy is there — but you have to believe.

Douglas Malloch.

One of the hardest lessons we have to learn in this life,
and one that many persons never learn,
is to see the divine, the celestial, the pure in the common,
the near at hand, — to see that heaven
lies about us here in this world.

John Burroughs

Optimism is a kind of heart stimulant — the digitalis of failure.

Elbert Hubbard

There are no hopeless situations; there are only men
who have grown hopeless about them.

Clare Boothe Luce

Happiness

Happiness is like a crystal,
Fair and exquisite and clear,
Broken in a million pieces,
Shattered, scattered far and near.
Now and then along life's pathway,
Lo! some shining fragments fall;
But there are so many pieces
No one ever finds them all.

You may find a bit of beauty,
Or an honest share of wealth,
While another just beside you
Gathers honor, love or health.
Vain to choose or grasp unduly,
Broken is the perfect ball;
And there are so many pieces
No one ever finds them all.

Yet the wise as on they journey
Treasure every fragment clear,
Fit them as they may together
Imaging the shattered sphere,
Learning ever to be thankful,
Though their share of it is small;
For it has so many pieces
No one ever finds them all.

Priscilla Leonard

There is something in the nature of things which the mind of man,
which reason, which human powers cannot effect, and certainly
that which produces this must be better than man.
What can this be but God.

Cicero

God evidently does not intend us all to be rich, or powerful,
or great, but He does intend us all to be friends.

Ralph Waldo Emerson

Hope is a thing with feathers
That perches in the soul,
And sings the tune without the words,
And never stops at all.

Emily Dickinson

And then one fine day, Mother's Day of 1957 to be exact, I received three potted geraniums, all gloriously swathed in crinkly tinfoil, for the sun porch. When they didn't, like their predecessors, wither and die within the week, I began to do a double-take. What was wrong? Was it possible that these geraniums really *liked* me?

It was a very giddy sensation, believe me. Quite went to my head. Maybe, I thought in my giddiness, I might even extend my green thumb prowess to the back yard? Sort of surprise my know-it-all neighbor next door? Have her look out her kitchen window one fine morning and be literally blinded by the riot of color I had wrought?

It also occurred to me that it might be very pleasant to saunter out in one's own garden . . . a straw basket over one's arm, clipping shears in hand . . . and gather a dew-drenched bouquet. (Never once had my neighbor urged me to pick her flowers, no matter how lavish my praise.) I was possibly also swayed by my fondness for British writers, all of whom . . . according to their personal journals . . . puttered happily around in (or at?) the "bottoms" of their gardens. (Have never looked up this expression but I presume it means the rear end of the lot? In my case, this would mean where the incinerator and the alley meet.) Anyhow, I was always coming across casual little observations like "A kingfisher haunts the stream that runs through the bottom of my garden" and, although bird-watching always left me cold, it certainly conjured up a pretty picture. Personally, I don't know *anyone* with a stream running through their back yard. All that runs through mine is a stream of neighborhood kids playing touch football.

But let us return, however reluctantly, to the American scene and stay there.

My approach to gardening can best be described as "furtive." To me, there seemed something faintly disreputable about a grown woman planting her first nasturtium seed at an age when she *should* be cross-breeding gardenias or something. It wasn't at all the same thing as the middle-aged women (the newspaper accounts of which left me steeped in admiration) who suddenly took up skin-diving, ran for Congress, or returned to high school to graduate with their grandchildren. *That* was inspiring. *This* was ridiculous. It was sort of like a woman . . . after twenty years of housekeeping . . .suddenly deciding to learn how to make French Toast.

Hence, I contented myself with a few discreet queries from my most intimate friends. What flowers were absolutely fool-proof? Could you really trust those colored packages of seeds at the supermarket? How did you know when the last frost was over? Did the seeds need any special nourishment to get going?

A seed was a seed, said my friends. All it needed, under God's providence, was sun and rain. "And be sure to keep stripping the flower beds," they added. "Especially the nasturtiums. They multiply faster that way."

They were much more explicit, though, about the *etiquette* of gardening. The sporting thing to do, they said, was to start from scratch; not buy any fledgling plants at the city market. However, it was quite acceptable . . . indeed, I gathered it was something like exchanging autographs in a school memory book . . . to receive shoots and bulbs from your friends and relatives. *Then* you had something to talk about when you conducted a guided tour around your yard. Like: "See that snowball bush over in the corner? Aunt Etta gave me a shoot off her bush . . . oh, it must've been ten years ago when I visited her in Sandusky . . . and just look at it now. It was touch and go, though, that first year. Real sickly. Then, it just seemed to catch hold. . . ."

This, then, seemed the essence of a *real* garden . . . memories, tradition, crucial illnesses, loving care . . . and it occurred to me that I, with my little 25¢ packages of seed, had a long row ahead of me. I mean, how did you get people to crash through with their donations? Should I send out gilt-edged invitations: "Mrs. Hasley, who has now taken up gardening, will receive donations from 3 to 6 next Sunday"? Anyhow, I'd better get the ground all churned up and ready . . .

I didn't mind the initial spadework at all. It was even quite pleasant, what with the two big shade trees protecting me from the sun and with the cunning little gophers to keep me entertained. They, the gophers, were really *so* cute the way they'd squat back on their haunches, arms folded, and look me coolly in the eye. At first, I couldn't decide whether it was a look of cool admiration (after all, I *was* breaking virgin ground) or a look of cool contempt, but now I think . . . yes, contempt.

Anyhow, those first weeks of anticipation were really among the happiest I'd known. I even, now that I'd rejoined the human race and become a gardener, started to read *The Home Garden* column (somewhat similar in tenor to Ann Landers) in the Chicago *Tribune* every morning.

Goodness, I thought comfortably, the problems *other* people were having! Here was a man in Gary whose elm trees were afflicted with phoem necrosis. Here was a man in Evansville whose corn, just as the ears ripened tenderly, was stripped by the gophers. (Solution: Take tin cans, remove both ends and place the cylinders over the ears like a suit of armor. A pretty little scene, I should think, provided you first removed the Campbell soup labels: the shining knights riding off to the great crusades.)

And while none of these problems were mine (indeed, I had none), I *could* join the spirited and even passionate controversy over our proposed national flower. Yeah, how *dare* that Senator So- and So propose the lowly corn tassel! It was unthinkable, with or without tin cans. And yet the rose, everyone's favorite by a sweeping majority, had already been selected by England. Did we dare, especially after the Suez Canal flare-up, create an international crisis by . . . ?

My head swimming from the various problems and decisions that faced us gardeners, I would then saunter out . . . master of the estate . . . to inspect the progress. Amazing! Man, that green fuzz was really coming along! (That is, it wasn't quite like the slogan said: Plant Manderville seeds and jump aside" — but it was *coming*.) It was even coming up in the children's abandoned sandbox where I, trustful to a degree, had patted down some aster seeds. (Asters, said the printed directions, did well in sandy soil.)

Finally after morning and night feedings, I felt that it (the green fuzz) was ready for transplanting. Carefully, and with all the skill of a laboratory technician, I replanted the fragile blobs of green life according to directions. Such as: "Petunias must be planted far apart, for they are a leafy plant that spreads rapidly."

Oh? Mine grew tall, skinny, spindly. To date, and it is now late August as I write this report, there have been exactly eleven blossoms. Pretty blossoms yes, but eleven. My score in the nasturtium bed, and I will swear this before a notary public, is one (1) blossom. The zinnias along the fence have done somewhat better (and so they should, if they have any pride at all, being Indiana's state flower), but it would be more effective, I think, if they bloomed at the same time. Not just one by one. As for the asters in the sandbox . . . well, they're an autumn flower, you know, and so I really can't tell as yet. But shouldn't they, by now, be more than two inches high?

"I think you've done real well," says my neighbor. "Everything looks real *tidy*. But if you want to raise flowers, you'll have to chop down those shade trees and kill the gophers."

And I, like Barbara Frietchie, say NEVER. There shall be no mayhem in *my* garden. Indeed, I would no more pick one of my poor blossoms (the question of gathering a bouquet does not arise) than I would behead one of my own children. Rather, to tell the truth, I feel quite tender toward my retarded garden. Can *it* help it that, two inches below the surface, there spreads a vast labyrinth of twisted tree roots, studded with young boulders, where dozens of cool-eyed gophers run up and down the corridors, munching nasturtium roots? You'd be retarded too.

Besides, I tell myself, masses of flowers can be so confusing, even rather vulgar, as versus a shy and delicate blossom standing out all by itself. Now you take the Japanese, and they're a really artistic race, with their floral arrangements: the loving appreciation of *a* lotus blossom, *a* twisted root, *a* single branch of pear blossoms. That is, the true nature lover . . . like the poet with his "O, flower in the crannied wall" . . . can read more meaning into a single and isolated miracle.

Lucile Hasley

Man is, properly speaking, based on Hope; he has no other possession but Hope.

Thomas Carlyle

57

Being optimistic after you get everything you want don't count.

Kin Hubbard

In green gardens, hidden away
From sight of revel and sound of strife,—
Here I have leisure to breathe and move,
And to do my work in a nobler way;
To sing my songs, and to say my say;
To dream my dreams, and to love my love;
To hold my faith, and to live my life,
Making the most of its shadowy day.

Violet Fane

On A Quiet Conscience

Close thine eyes, and sleep secure;
Thy soul is safe, thy body sure.
He that guards thee, he that keeps,
Never slumbers, never sleeps.
A quiet conscience in the breast
Has only peace, has only rest,
The wisest and the mirth of kings
Are out of tune unless she sings:
Then close thine eyes in peace and sleep secure,
No sleep so sweet as thine, no rest so sure.

Charles I of England

Hope is itself a species of happiness, and, perhaps,
the chief happiness which this world affords.

Samuel Johnson

Truth is wherever you decide to face it.

John Berry

The greatest homage we can pay to truth is to use it.

Ralph Waldo Emerson

One of the many things nobody ever tells you about middle age
is that it is such a nice change from being young.

Dorothy Canfield Fisher

There is nothing so strong or safe in an emergency of life
as the simple truth.

Charles Dickens

It is a most exciting thing
To take a garden in the Spring:

To wonder what its borders hold;
What secrets lurk beneath the mold?

What kinds of roses you have got;
Whether the lilac blooms, or not.

Whether the peach tree, on the wall,
Has ever had a peach at all. . . .

It is a most exciting thing
To take a garden in the Spring;

And live in such delicious doubt,
Until the final flower is out.

Reginald Arkell

Before us is a future all unknown, a path
     untrod;
Beside us a friend well loved and known—
     That friend is God.

Unknown

Whatever a man's age, he can reduce it several years
by putting a bright-colored flower in his buttonhole.

Mark Twain

Hope is a much better stimulant of life than any happiness.

Friedrich Nietzsche

Truth generally is kindness, but where the two diverge and
collide, kindness should override truth.

Samuel Butler

To me old age is always fifteen years older than I am.

Bernard Baruch

If it weren't for faith, there would be no living in this world;
we couldn't even eat hash.

Josh Billings

Song

The year's at the spring,
And day's at the morn;
Morning's at seven;
The hillside's dew-pearled;
The lark's on the wing;
The snail's on the thorn;
God's in his heaven—
All's right with the world.

Robert Browning

To profit from good advice requires more wisdom
than to give it.

John Churton Collins

Heaven must be in me before I can be in heaven.

Leland Stanford

The exact contrary of what is generally believed
is often the truth.

Jean de La Bruyère

Youth is happy because it has the ability to see beauty.
Anyone who keeps the ability to see beauty never grows old.

Franz Kafka

Hills Ahead

The hills ahead look hard and steep and high
And often we behold them with a sigh;
But as we near them level grows the road.
We find on every slope with every load
The climb is not so steep, the top so far,
The hills ahead look harder than they are.

And so it is with troubles though they seem so great
That men complain and fear and hesitate;
Less difficult the journey than we dreamed
It never proves as hard as once it seemed,
There never comes a task, a hill, a day
But as we near it — easier the way.

Douglas Malloch

The Footpath to Peace

To be glad of life, because it gives you the chance to love and to
work and to play and to look up at the stars; to be satisfied with your
possessions, but not contented with yourself until you have made
the best of them; to despise nothing in the world except falsehood
and meanness, and to fear nothing except cowardice; to be governed
by your admirations rather than by your disgusts; to covet nothing
that is your neighbor's except his kindness of heart and gentleness
of manner; to think seldom of your enemies, often of your friends
and every day of Christ; and to spend as much time as you can with
body and with spirit, in God's out-of-doors — these are the little
guideposts on the footpath of peace.

Henry van Dyke

Hope and patience are two sovereign remedies for all,
the surest reposals, the softest cushions to lean on in adversity.

Robert Burton

The natural flights of the human mind are not from pleasure
to pleasure, but from hope to hope.

Samuel Johnson

Wisdom

It was a night of early spring,
   The winter-sleep was scarcely broken;
Around us shadows and the wind
   Listened for what was never spoken.

Though half a score of years are gone,
   Spring comes as sharply now as then—
But if we had it all to do
   It would be done the same again.

It was a spring that never came;
   But we have lived enough to know
That what we never have, remains;
   It is the things we have that go.

Sara Teasdale

Human Need

Courage we need for this life of ours,
Courage, calmness, power;
Glee in the present which children own,
Hope for the coming hour.

Underneath, and all the time,
A warm pulse, beating
To Nature's beauty, loved one's rhythm,
The springtime urge repeating.

What will give us courage deep,
Joy in the things that are?
The true and lasting love of friends
For us, will go most far.

Madeline Benedict

When all else is lost, the future still remains.

C. N. Bovee

Earth has no sorrow heaven cannot heal.

Thomas Moore

Ode

We are the music-makers,
And we are the dreamers of dreams,
Wandering by lone sea-breakers,
And sitting by desolate streams;

World-losers and world-forsakers,
On whom the pale moon gleams;
Yet we are the movers and shakers
Of the world forever, it seems.

With wonderful deathless ditties
We build up the world's great cities,
And out of a fabulous story
We fashion an empire's glory.

One man with a dream, at pleasure,
Shall go forth and conquer a crown
And three with a new song's measure
Can trample an empire down.

We, in the ages lying
In the buried past of the earth,
Built Nineveh with our sighing,
And Babel itself with our mirth;

And o'erthrew them with prophesying
To the old of the new world's worth;
For each age is a dream that is dying,
Or one that is coming to birth.

Arthur William Edgar O'Shaughnessy

Be not afraid of life. Believe that life is worth living
and your belief will help create the fact.

William James

How poor are they who have not patience!
What wound did ever heal, but by degrees?

William Shakespeare

O World, Thou Chooseth Not The Better Part

O world, thou chooseth not the better part!
It is not wisdom to be only wise,
And on the inward vision close the eyes,
But it is wisdom to believe the heart.
Columbus found a world, and had no chart
Save one that faith deciphered in the skies;
To trust the soul's invincible surmise
Was all his science and his only art.
Our knowledge is a torch of smoky pine
That lights the pathway but one step ahead
Across a void of mystery and dread.
Bid, then, the tender light of faith to shine
By which alone the mortal heart is led
Unto the thinking of the thought divine.

George Santayana

Invictus

Out of the night that covers me,
Black as the Pit from pole to pole,
I thank whatever gods may be
For my unconquerable soul.

In the fell clutch of circumstance
I have not winced nor cried aloud.
Under the bludgeonings of chance
My head is bloody, but unbowed.

Beyond this place of wrath and tears
Looms but the Horror of the shade,
And yet the menace of the years
Finds and shall find me unafraid.

It matters not how strait the gate,
How charged with punishments the scroll,
I am the master of my fate:
I am the captain of my soul.

William Ernest Henley

64

With God nothing shall be impossible.

Luke 1:37

Keep your face to the sunshine and you cannot see the shadow.

Helen Keller

A Little Song of Life

Glad that I live am I;
That the sky is blue;
Glad for the country lanes,
And the fall of dew.

After the sun the rain,
After the rain the sun;
This is the way of life,
Till the work be done.

All that we need to do,
Be we low or high,
Is to see that we grow
Nearer the sky.

Lizette Woodworth Reese

Unsubdued

I have hoped, I have planned, I have striven,
To the will I have added the deed;
The best that was in me I've given,
I have prayed, but the gods would not heed.

I have dared and reached only disaster,
I have battled and broken my lance;
I am bruised by a pitiless master
That the weak and the timid call Chance.

I am old, I am bent, I am cheated
Of all that Youth urged me to win;
But name me not with the defeated,
Tomorrow again, I begin.

Samuel S. E. Kiser

'Whatsoever Things Are True'

Whatsoever things are true,
whatsoever things are honest,
whatsoever things are just,
whatsoever things are pure,
whatsoever things are lovely,
whatsoever things are of good report;
if there be any virtue,
and if there be any praise,
think on these things.

Phillippians 4:8

Say Not

Say not, the struggle nought availeth,
The labor and the wounds are vain,
The enemy faints not, nor faileth,
And as things have been they remain.

If hopes were dupes, fears may be liars;
It may be, in yon smoke concealed,
Your comrades chase e'en now the fliers,
And, but for you, possess the field.

For while the tired waves, vainly breaking,
Seem here no painful inch to gain,
Far back, through creeks and inlets making,
Comes silent, flooding in, the main.

And not by eastern windows only,
When daylight comes, comes in the light;
In front, the sun climbs slow, how slowly!
But westward, look, the land is bright!

A. H. Clough

Be such a man, and live such a life, that if
every man were such as you, the earth would be
God's paradise.

Phillips Brooks

66

A Turn In The Road

Just a turn in the road,
A turn to the right,
Then, you'll find a pathway—
A beautiful sight.

Your pathway to heaven!
You can't go astray;
You'll see a bright starlet
To light up your way.

All hope will be reborn—
New vistas unfold.
Push on to your mountain—
Push on to your goal.

Just keep right on striving,
Though heavy the load,
And you'll come at last
To the turn in the road.

A turn in the road
Where life starts anew.
A turn in the road
Where dreams will come true.

So, lift up your head
And laugh at your load;
At last you will come
To the turn in the road.

                        Hilda Gross Feinblum

Two men look out through the same bars:
One sees mud, and one the stars.

                        Frederick Langbridge

Courage and perserverance have a magical talisman,
before which difficulties disappear and obstacles
vanish into air.

                        John Quincy Adams

Reaching Our Goal

Perhaps the day may come, oh anxious world
When we, with gallant hope, will win life's fame.
Till then, we'll climb the ladder, step by step,
Striving till we've reached our highest aim.

Never give up the hope that we shall win
The temporal joys of love and life unknown.
If we but walk the straight and narrow way,
We'll build ourselves a shining stepping stone.

Sara Anderson

I Never Saw a Moor

I never saw a moor,
I never saw the sea;
Yet know I how the heather looks,
And what a wave must be.

I never spoke with God,
Nor visited in heaven;
Yet certain am I of the spot
As if the chart were given.

Emily Dickinson

I Heard a Bird Sing

I heard a bird sing
In the dark of December
A magical thing
And sweet to remember.

"We are nearer to Spring
Than we were in September,"
I heard a bird sing
In the dark of December.

Oliver Herford

God sometimes puts us on our back so that we may look upward.

Unknown

Most of the shadows of this life are caused
by standing in our own sunshine.

Ralph Waldo Emerson

It is better to light one small candle than
to curse the darkness.

Confucius

Life affords no higher pleasure than that of
surmounting difficulties, passing from one step
of success to another, forming new wishes, and
seeing them gratified. He that labors in any great
or laudable undertaking has his fatigues first
supported by hope, and afterwards rewarded by joy.

Samuel Johnson

It's not life that counts but the fortitude you bring into it.

John Galsworthy

Never a tear bedims the eye
That time and patience will not dry.

Bret Harte

All I have seen teaches me to trust the Creator for all I have not seen.

Ralph Waldo Emerson

Let us be of good cheer, remembering that
the misfortunes hardest to bear are those
which never happen.

James Russell Lowell

Ask, and it shall be given you; seek, and ye shall
find; knock, and it shall be opened unto you.

Matthew 7:7

Acknowledgments

The editor and the publisher have made every effort to trace the ownership of all copyrighted material and to secure permission from holders of such material. In the event of any question arising as to the use of any material the publisher and editor, while expressing regret for inadvertent error, will be pleased to make the necessary corrections in future printings. Thanks are due to the following authors, publishers, publications and agents for permission to use the material indicated.

BARRIE & JENKINS LTD., for selection by Reginold Arkell from *Green Fingers*.

ALBERT AND CHARLES BONI, INC., for a quotation by Ambrose Bierce from *Devil's Dictionary*.

MAURICE CHEVALIER, for two one-line quotations with his permission.

WILLIAM B. EERDMANS PUBLISHING COMPANY, for "Feeling Low" by Harold E. Kohn.

FARRAR, STRAUS & GIROUX, INC., for three quotations from *The Life and Times of Kim Hubbard* by Fred C. Kelly (Copyright, 1951, by Fred C. Kelly).

HARPER & ROW, PUBLISHERS, for an abridged letter — Nov. 28, 1969 — "My Dear, Dear Livy:" from *The Love Letters of Mark Twain* edited by Dixon Wecter (Copyright, 1947, 1949, by The Mark Twain Company); quotations from *The New Book of Unusual Quotations* by Rudolf Flesch.

SYDNEY HARRIS AND PUBLISHERS-HALL SYNDICATE, for one quotation from the "Chicago Daily News."

HARTFORD, HARTMOOR HOUSE, for quotations from *A Treasury of The Art of Living* edited by Sidney Greenberg.

WILLIAM HEINEMANN LTD., PUBLISHERS, for the passage from *The Brothers Karamazov* by Feodor Dostoyevsky, translated by Constance Garnett.

HOLT, RINEHART AND WINSTON, INC., for a quotation by Will Cuppy from *The Decline and Fall of Practically Everybody*, edited by Fred Feldkamp (Copyright, 1950, by Fred Feldkamp); "A Little Song of Life" from *A Wayside Lute* by Lizette Woodworth Reese.

HOLT, RINEHART AND WINSTON, INC., JONATHAN CAPE LTD., EDWARD CONNERY LATHEM, and THE ESTATE OF ROBERT FROST, for "The Road Not Taken" from *The Poetry of Robert Frost*, edited by Edward Connery Lathem (Copyright 1916, © 1969 by Holt, Rinehart and Winston, Inc., copyright 1944 by Robert Frost.)

HOUGHTON MIFFLIN COMPANY, for "A Love Letter, John Chapman to his Wife" from *John Jay Chapman and His Letters* edited by M. A. DeWolfe Howe; "Opal" from *The Complete Poetical Works of Amy Lowell*; a quotation from *The Light of Day* by John Burroughs.

ALFRED A. KNOPF, INC., for a quotation from *The Journal of Andre Gide* (Copyright, 1947, 1951, by Alfred A. Knopf, Inc.); a quotation from *Prejudices: First Series* by H. L. Mencken (Copyright, 1924, by Alfred A. Knopf, Inc.).

J. B. LIPPINCOTT COMPANY, for "Reading Aloud" from *Chimneysmoke* by Christopher Morley (Copyright, 1921, renewal, 1949, by Christopher Morley).